The year is 1917 and the people of Russia have been driven beyond despair. For centuries they have endured the cruel repression and exploitation of the ruthless tsarist tyranny; for centuries their every striving for freedom and even a modestly tolerable standard of living has been smothered beneath the weight of a greedy and reactionary ruling class. To these age-old woes, in 1914 has been added the crushing burden of Russia's participation in World War I. In this holocaust the ill-armed, poorly led, all-but-untrained Russian armies have suffered endless catastrophe. Millions of Russian soldiers have perished and now they are deserting by the thousands.

In March, 1917, in one gigantic, nearly spontaneous convulsion, the Russian people shrug off the chains of tsarism. But the new democratic Provisional Government, led by liberals and socialists, is unable to provide what the masses of Russian peasants and workers desperately need: land, bread, and immediate peace. By promising these things, the Russian Bolshevik party (Communist), led by brilliant revolutionaries such as Lenin and Trotsky, is able, through months of upheaval, to win the support of the people. In November, 1917, the Bolsheviks stage another uprising which wins them control of the nation. The Russian people choose to "break a new path into the future."

PRINCIPALS

KARL MARX & FRIEDRICH ENGELS, German political philosophers who created the theoretical foundations of communism during the mid-nineteenth century.

NICHOLAS II, weak-willed and autocratic tsar of Russia.

ALEXANDRA (formerly Princess Alix), Nicholas's wife, a religious fanatic.

GREGORY RASPUTIN, a half-crazed, cynically fake "holy man" whose influence over the royal family and their autocratic government was complete.

ALEXANDER KERENSKY, liberal socialist premier of the Russian Provisional Government.

VLADIMIR ULYANOV (LENIN), pragmatic, totally dedicated leader of the Russian Bolshevik (Communist) party.

LEV BRONSTEIN (TROTSKY), brilliant Marxist revolutionary, Lenin's principal lieutenant in 1917.

GENERAL LAVR KORNILOV, commander of the Russian armies in 1917 who plotted to destroy the revolution and reimpose tsarist rule.

GEORGI PLEKHANOV, founder of the Russian Social Democratic party from which Lenin's Bolsheviks later split.

A view of the Winter Palace in Petrograd, 1917.

THE FALL OF THE WINTER PALACE

NOVEMBER 1917
Old Russia's Tsardom Is Swept Away by Bolshevik Revolution

By Robert Goldston

A World Focus Book

FRANKLIN WATTS, INC.
845 Third Avenue
New York, New York 10022

The author and publisher wish to acknowledge the helpful
editorial suggestions of Professor Loren R. Graham,
Russian Institute, Columbia University in the City of New York.

All photos courtesy Charles Phelps Cushing.

Contents

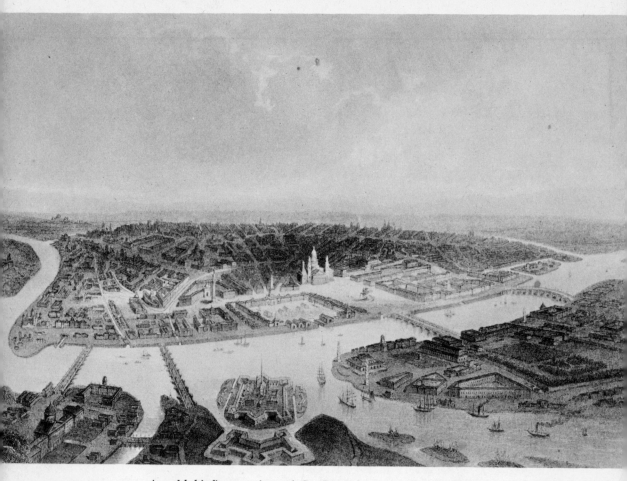

An old bird's-eye view of St. Petersburg on the Neva River during the eighteenth century. City's name was later changed to Petrograd.

Prologue:
White Twilight

November 7, 1917, was on the surface a day like many others in Petrograd, a Russian city grown used to deprivation, war, civil disorders, and revolution. The broad avenues, the imperial buildings, the bridges over the Neva River, the outlying workers' quarters, the Fortress of Saints Peter and Paul — all were mantled with snow. The sky was sheathed with leaden gray clouds, and an icy wind blowing off the Baltic Sea searched the streets. Pedestrians leaned into this wind, wrapped in furs if they were rich, swathed in rags if they were poor. Most of the pedestrians were women, old men, and youngsters; the young men, aside from Petrograd-stationed guards regiments and essential munitions factory workers, were at the front as they had been for three years now, fighting gallantly but hopelessly against far better-armed and better-led German and Austrian armies. There was little traffic on the streets; only official or military vehicles could get gasoline, and the horse-drawn cabs had grown fewer as the horses were slaughtered for meat. Outside grocery stores, butcher shops, and bakeries long lines of people patiently waited in hopes of getting their meager daily rations.

This was Petrograd (a Russian form of the words "Saint Petersburg"), the imperial city constructed by decree of Tsar Peter the Great at the beginning of the eighteenth century. This was the city that was to have served as Peter's "window on the

1

West," a symbol to turn the attention of the Russian people toward European industrial progress and away from "Asiatic barbarism." Raised from the icy and pestilential marshes that bordered the Baltic Sea, the building of Petrograd cost the lives of hundreds of thousands of laborers — one for every stone in the city, it was said. This was the capital of all the vast expanse of Russia, from the frozen wastes of the Arctic to the sun-baked deserts of Turkestan, from Poland to the Sea of Japan — more than one-sixth of the land surface of the entire world.

The stones of Petrograd had changed but little since the days of Peter the Great. Of course, there were little red flags stuck into the hands of the many tsarist monuments in the city, and long red cloth streamers hung down the fronts of most government buildings. These were outward signs that although the stones of the city might not have changed, the hearts of its citizens had. For there was no longer a tsar in Petrograd; he and his family and the government he had headed and the aristocracy that had surrounded him had been swept away by a revolution the previous March. Then, exasperated beyond endurance by the tryannical, fumbling, and utterly corrupt autocracy that had oppressed and exploited them for untold centuries, their patience finally exhausted by the senseless holocaust of a world war in which they perished by the millions, the people of Russia, led by the citizens of Petrograd, had risen up spontaneously and shaken off the old regime in one mighty convulsion.

Those revolutionary March days, during which many died, should have ushered in a new era, most of the people of Petrograd thought. The whole structure of tsarist oppression had been dismantled; Russia was ruled now by a democratic Provisional Government composed of leaders of many political parties.

During the revolutionary March days Red Guards demonstrate in Petrograd.

Power was in the hands of an elective assembly, the *Duma*, and in the hands of local, regional, and national councils of workers, peasants, and soldiers — the *Soviets.* Through and to these bodies the national will was made unmistakably clear; better hours, wages, and conditions for industrial workers, land for the peasants, political democracy, and, above all, an immediate end to the agony of the war.

But something seemed to have gone wrong following the March revolution. Somehow, the new government, for all its fine words, had not been able to meet the people's demands. And because of this, unknown to many — perhaps even to most — of the citizens of Petrograd, a military-political drama of world-shaking consequences was unfolding in their city on November 7, 1917 ("October Revolution," according to the old-style Russian calendar).

A Meeting at the Winter Palace

At about noon on that fateful day, the ministers of the Provisional Government met in the ornate Malachite Chamber of the former tsar's Winter Palace. It was not a happy meeting. The ministers had assembled there during the early hours of the morning in search of refuge. For despite the appearance of calm and "business as usual" in the streets of Petrograd, they knew that the Red Guard, a ragged but armed and determined "people's militia," led by the Bolshevik, or Communist party, had been busy all night occupying government offices, telephone and telegraph exchanges, public utility centers, railway stations, bridges, police stations — every key or commanding position in the city. The Bolshevik party, apparently with the support, or at least acquiescence, of the Petrograd garrison and the people of the city, was even then in the process of seizing power from the Provisional Government.

The premier of this government, Alexander Kerensky, did not attend the ministers' deliberations in the Winter Palace; he had already fled Petrograd in a car requisitioned from the American Embassy. Presumably Kerensky was on his way to the battlefront to raise troops to put down the Bolshevik uprising.

If that was true, the ministers reflected, Kerensky had better hurry. All day long they watched as detachments of men in ragged, soiled work clothes, armed with rifles, pistols, and occa-

5

Petrograd, November, 1917. The Duma of the Provisional Government meets in its last session.

sionally machine guns, took up positions around the edges of the great square in front of the palace. During the afternoon, seven gray warships of the Russian Baltic Fleet steamed slowly up the river Neva and anchored. That their crews were Bolshevik-led was proven (if there had been any doubts) when the great guns of the warships slowly swung to point directly at the Winter Palace.

To defend this massive pile of gray stone masonry, the Provisional Government had been able to muster only a few companies of military cadets, mere boys hastily summoned from local training schools; a few groups of soldierless officers; and a volunteer women's battalion. It seemed to the ministers that they had been utterly deserted.

"We wandered," one of them later recalled, "through the gigantic mousetrap, meeting occasionally, either all together or in small groups, for brief conversations — condemned people, lonely, abandoned by all. . . . Around us vacancy, within us

Revolutionaries parade through the streets of Petrograd in November, 1917.

vacancy, and in this grew up the soulless courage of placid indifference."

Yet there was still hope. Perhaps the people of Petrograd or a regiment of troops loyal to the government would intervene. Perhaps, even now, divisions of battle-hardened veterans from the nearby front (the Germans were only a few dozen miles from the city) were hurrying back to save them at Kerensky's command. When, at 6:00 P.M., the Bolshevik forces facing the palace sent in an ultimatum demanding its surrender, the government ministers refused — and moved to a room deeper within the building.

Then, at precisely 9:00 P.M., a heavy cannon spoke from the Fortress of Saints Peter and Paul. It was answered by a naval gun booming from the cruiser *Aurora* anchored in the Neva. . . .

The Prison of Nations

The drama unfolding in Petrograd in 1917 was not accidental; neither was it merely the action of a group of willful men. It was the all-but-inevitable result of forces beyond the control of any man or party; it was the culmination of centuries of history.

Those centuries had been long and cruel for the Russian people. They had never, in their entire history, known freedom; instead they had known only slavery, tyranny, and conquest. For longer than men could remember, the semisavage tribes of Central Asia had swept westward over the broad Russian plains in destructive tides. The most shattering of these migratory invasions had been that of the Mongols in A.D. 1237. Slaughtering entire populations, razing cities and towns, stripping the countryside, and enslaving the survivors, the Mongols fastened a grip on Russia that lasted for more than two hundred years.

While western Europe climbed slowly out of its "dark ages," while nations began to emerge from the chaos left by the wreckage of the Roman Empire, while men's minds in the West were illuminated by a Renaissance of learning and science, Russia slowly and painfully battled to drive out the conquerors from the East. Under the leadership of the Princes of Muscovy (petty nobles controlling the lands around the town of Moscow) the costly wars of reconquest ended in Russian expulsion of the Mongols from their central territories in the sixteenth century. In A.D. 1533 Ivan IV ("the Terrible") became prince of Muscovy

9

Ivan IV ("the Terrible"), Tsar of All the Russians.

and fourteen years later he was able to proclaim himself Tsar ("Caesar") of All the Russians. Ivan and his successors (after a period of civil wars the crown passed to the Romanov family) fastened so tight a yoke on the backs of the Russian people that it seemed nothing could ever shake it.

By tsarist decree the people of Russia were, during the seventeenth century, divided and frozen into rigid classes. Peasants were bound to the land (and to the aristocratic owners of the land) on pain of death; townspeople were bound to their villages and cities. The independence of the nobility and of the Russian Orthodox Church was crushed. In all the broad land of Russia only the tsar and his ever-growing government bureaucracy exercised power. Opposition to this autocracy (rule of one man) was met by a vast police force and punished by imprison-

10

Old print of a typical Russian rural town in 1809 reflects the stark poverty of the Russian people during the Napoleonic era.

ment, exile to the frozen wastes of Siberia, or execution. When police measures were not sufficient (as in the case of sporadic peasant uprisings) the army and the cossacks (special mounted warriors fiercely loyal to their patron, the tsar) would be used to massacre the people.

The overwhelming majority of the Russian people worked

A portrait of Peter the Great (Tsar Peter I) of Russia.

Catherine the Great, empress of Russia.

land that was not theirs in conditions of appalling poverty as serfs (semislaves). They were looked upon by their aristocratic masters and by the tsarist autocracy as animals. Indeed, it was as animals that Peter the Great had used them to build Petrograd; it was as animals that Catherine the Great drove them to the Crimean Campaign in 1768; it was as animals that Alexander I whipped them to defeat Napoleon's invasion of Russia in 1812.

But as the Russian armies of serfs led by nobles flooded across Europe at the close of the Napoleonic Wars, Western ideas of freedom and progress ebbed back and began to penetrate the empire of the tsars. When Alexander I died in 1825, a group of army officers and petty nobles tried to overthrow the autocracy and replace it with some ill-defined form of parliamentary democracy. Known as the Decembrists (from the month in which they struck), these men were quickly and ruthlessly arrested, condemned, and punished by Alexander's son, Nicholas I, the new tsar. Frightened, nevertheless, by this attempt on his crown, Tsar Nicholas I reviewed the ancient and already tyrannical laws of his empire — in order to make them harsher still! He issued a barrage of imperial decrees that further degraded the Russian people and tightened government control over all aspects of Russian life. Schools, newspapers, universities, the army, even the already corrupt and reactionary Orthodox Church: all felt the heavy hand of repression. In the middle of the nineteenth century — after revolutions had swept America, France, and even the backward countries of South America — Russian society remained hopelessly repressive and reactionary.

But repression at home did not pay dividends abroad. Nicholas I found that his armies of illiterate, humiliated serfs could

Tsar Alexander I of Russia.

Tsar Nicholas I of Russia.

no longer stand their ground before the military organization and firepower of modern foes. When Russia suffered a humiliating defeat at the hands of England and France during the Crimean War of 1853–56, it became apparent, even to the most reactionary elements of the autocracy, that changes would have to be made — not in the name of liberty, but of simple efficiency.

Nicholas I's son, Alexander II, undertook these reforms. He eased state censorship and control of schools, newspapers, the judicial system, and the army. Above all, he liberated the serfs, transforming them, at a stroke of the imperial pen, from feudal slaves to "free" peasants. Of course these "free" peasants remained in bondage through debt to local landowners — and they continued to freeze, starve, wear sandals made of the bark of trees, live in mud-and-wattle huts, and suffer the lash for any

14

protest. And if government control of Russian thought, as expressed in schools, newspapers, and the Church, was somewhat relaxed, yet the prisons remained full of dissidents, hundreds of "subversives" were shipped yearly to Siberia, and the power of the police continued to grow until that institution became almost a state within the state. And if the army was reformed and modernized, it was steadily employed — in the conquest of the backward peoples and tribes of Central and southern Asia, until at last the tsar's power reached the frontiers of India and China and the shores of the far Pacific. The mighty empire that was a tyranny for Russians was literally a prison of nations for non-Russians.

Yet the might of empire, the power of the autocracy, and the meager reforms he instituted could not protect the tsar. On March 13, 1881, while he was driving in his royal coach, Alexander II's life was ended by a bomb tossed at him by a band of

Tsar Alexander II of Russia.

Tsar Alexander III of Russia.

desperate revolutionaries. His successor, Alexander III, could execute the assassins — and later execute other bands of conspirators — but he could never manage to control the rising waves of discontent that grew ever stronger during the last half of the nineteenth century. It was in a spirit of desperate determination to preserve his crown that Nicholas II inherited the throne in 1894 upon the death of his father.

But where the new tsar's parents and ancestors had displayed personal strength and determination, Nicholas's character proved to be that of an indecisive weakling. The charlatan monk Gregory Rasputin, as a matter of fact, once remarked that the tsar "lacked insides." Count Sergei Witte, a hardheaded administrator of the autocracy, later wrote: " 'I wish it; therefore it must be' — that motto appeared in all the activities of this weak ruler, who only through weakness did all the things which characterized his reign — a wholesale shedding of more or less innocent blood, for the most part without aim."

To help him bear the burdens of the tsardom, Nicholas had chosen for a wife Princess Alix, a German-born granddaughter of Britain's Queen Victoria. Perhaps because of her foreign birth, Alix filled the vacancy of her royal life with an increasingly fanatical devotion to the Russian Orthodox Church — a devotion that quickly slipped into deep and mindless superstition. She surrounded herself with all manner of fake "holy men" and mystics — until at last she fell under the sway of the degenerate,

Nicholas II, last emperor and tsar of Russia.

The last tsar of Russia with Tsarina Alexandra and their children. At his parents' feet sits the Tsarevitch Alexis, who suffered from hemophilia. In the back row (left to right) are the Grand Duchesses Anastasia, Tatiana, and Olga. Marie is at her father's left.

half-crazed monk Gregory Rasputin. So great was Rasputin's hold over the tsarina (she believed that only he could preserve the life of her son, Alexis, who suffered from hemophilia, the sickness causing uncontrollable bleeding) and so great was the tsarina's hold over Nicholas that this semiliterate monk appointed and fired government ministers and made decisions affecting the fate of the empire. But that fate was increasingly being decided by forces over which neither Nicholas nor Rasputin had any control.

By the end of the nineteenth century, Russian conquests in the Far East and penetration of Manchuria and Korea, at the expense of the decayed and all-but-defenseless Chinese Empire, had aroused the antagonism of a newly industrialized, militant,

Russia's "mad monk" Rasputin is pictured here bestowing his blessing upon his women disciples.

and expansionist Japan. When Nicholas and his advisers (who held the "upstart" and "heathen" yellow races in contempt) refused to negotiate, the Japanese made war. In a surprise attack on February 8, 1904, they destroyed Russia's Far Eastern Fleet at anchor in the naval base of Port Arthur. Later they destroyed Russia's Baltic Fleet, which had been sent on a suicidal mission halfway around the world to give battle. Within months Japan had conquered Manchuria and Korea and reduced the big Russian bases at Port Arthur and Vladivostok. At a peace conference held in September, 1905, at Portsmouth, New Hampshire, under the patronage of President Theodore Roosevelt, the Russians admitted defeat. But the loss of territory and influence in the Far East was as nothing to the disasters faced by the tsarist autocracy at home.

"Bloody Sunday"

The Russian people themselves had no interest in Tsar Nicholas's war. They viewed it, correctly, as just another "natural" catastrophe. Still, they had to suffer the consequences of it. They perished by the thousands in terribly mismanaged battles at the front, and at home they starved when wartime profiteering and plain inefficiency cut off food supplies from the big cities. In January, 1905, the Petrograd metalworkers, led by a fiery priest named Father Gapon, went on strike. They were striking not for an increase in wages, but simply for the payment of wages due them.

On January 22, 1905, some two hundred thousand workers and their families, led by Father Gapon, massed before the Winter Palace, confident that if they could only make themselves heard by the tsar — who was known as their cherished "little father" — that ruler would remedy their wrongs. But the tsar was not in the Winter Palace that day. Nicholas had fled with his family to a nearby royal estate. He left behind him a welcoming party of police and cossacks. When the huge crowd pressed into the square before the palace, these armed men opened fire at point-blank range, killing hundreds of men, women, and children. The workers fled and Father Gapon went into hiding. Later he sent the tsar a letter: "The innocent blood of workers, their wives and children lies forever between thee, oh soul-destroyer, and the Russian people. . . ."

21

Father Gapon (with cross) is shown here in 1905 at the opening of a Russian factory-workers' union.

"Bloody Sunday," as the Petrograd massacre was called, triggered a wave of angry strikes and protest movements throughout Russia. When these riots could not be controlled by the police, the tsarist autocracy called in troops — only to find that the armies, demoralized by their defeat in the Far East, could not be relied upon. Moreover, units of the Black Sea Fleet mutinied. Councils, or Soviets, of workers took over the administration of Moscow, Petrograd, Kiev, and other large cities. Peasants burned manor houses and attempted to seize the land. The revolutionaries received weapons smuggled in from America, where

22

the author Mark Twain summed up the American view by saying: "If such a government cannot be overthrown otherwise than by dynamite, then thank God for dynamite."

Under this mounting pressure, Tsar Nicholas had to give in. He promised the people land reform, reform of the administration, the establishment of a parliamentary democracy (under himself as tsar), and even a constitution. Gradually the violence subsided; gradually the tsar regained control over his regiments and the navy. By New Year's Day of 1906, the revolution was over — and the tsar was again strong enough to imprison, execute, and exile the revolutionary leaders. He was also strong enough to be able to go back on his word. He repealed most of his promises about reforms and constitutions — and where he kept them (as he did when he permitted the gathering of a Duma, or parliament), he made sure they were meaningless. Thus the tsar and the Russian ruling classes settled back after 1905, certain that their world had been made safe again — and, indeed, that it would last forever.

But once again, outside events were to intervene. World War I, which broke out in the summer of 1914, was caused, in no small part, by the stupid and vainglorious foreign policy of the Russian autocracy. Nicholas II looked upon himself as the protector of all European Slavs, and hence he had guaranteed the independence of various small Balkan nations such as Serbia and Bulgaria. When, in July of 1914, Serbian-backed terrorists assassinated the Archduke Franz Ferdinand, heir to the Austrian throne, Austria issued a severe ultimatum to Serbia. Despite Serbian acceptance of most of the provisions of the ultimatum, Austria declared war on the small Slav state. Russia immediately mobilized her forces along the Austrian frontier. Austria's ally,

Russian troops are shown here retreating in Galicia in 1916.

Germany, then mobilized her armies. But Russia was allied to France, and when Germany mobilized, so did the French. England had an unwritten understanding with France. And so the armies marched into World War I.

Although World War I came as a stunning surprise to the Russian people, they supported it enthusiastically enough at first. Frustrations at home were taken out on the hated enemy at the front. But the terribly underequipped Russian armies (in many regiments there was only one rifle for every two or three men), led in some cases by incompetent generals, marched from disaster to disaster. Thousands of soldiers lost their lives in needless

24

holocausts as German forces penetrated deeper and deeper into western Russia. Retreat followed retreat, and demoralization spread. Soon the Russian troops were deserting by the thousands. And all the attendant suffering of the home front — food and fuel shortages, the breakdown of transportation and communications — grew to nightmarish proportions.

Government ministers, wealthy manufacturers, aristocratic landowners, and their representatives in the all but powerless Duma grew alarmed as the suffering of the people increased. They begged Tsar Nicholas to initiate reforms. But the tsar would listen to none of this. Fixing on the monk Gregory Rasputin as the "evil genius" of the tsardom, certain aristocrats (including members of the royal family) murdered the fake holy man on the last day of 1916. In doing this, they thought to force the tsar into granting reforms and to appease the growing wrath of the people. But after nearly four centuries of tsarist autocracy the time for reform had passed. It was not of reform that the Russian masses dreamed, but of revolution.

The Revolutionists

During the last half of the nineteenth century, a revolutionary movement had slowly been gathering force behind the seemingly indestructible facade of the absolutist empire of tsarist Russia. The revolutionists, who were coping with total tyranny, explored various political philosophies, attempting to find a solution to Russia's problems. Some placed their faith in parliamentary democracy — with or without a tsar as figurehead. Others looked forward to the creation of a state in which the industrial workers would wield all economic and political power. Some placed their faith in the peasantry. And some, influenced by the romantic and violent personality of Mikhail Bakunin, advocated the abolition of any kind of government at all.

Since Russia remained overwhelmingly a peasant land, the largest and, in the countryside, most popular revolutionary groups were those which advocated true peasant liberation, the seizure of the land, and the creation of a new society which would be built upon and cater to peasant aspirations. Toward the close of the nineteenth century, these groups united to form the Social Revolutionary party which was, until after the revolution, to remain Russia's largest political party. But Social Revolutionary aims were both limited and, in an increasingly industrialized society, unrealistic. Nor did it seem that the dispersed and unwieldy masses of Russian peasants could ever be welded into a decisive revolutionary striking force.

26

Of all the revolutionary groups in Russia, the one which seemed to promise most effective action was the Social Democratic party, founded secretly in 1898 by Georgi Plekhanov. Plekhanov was a student and follower of the political-economic philosophy of communism as developed by Karl Marx and Friedrich Engels — indeed, he had made the first translations of Marxist writing into the Russian language.

Marx and Engels, two German political philosophers who spent most of their lives in exile in England, had attempted, through a study of history and economics, to formulate answers to the pressing problems created by the Industrial Revolution. They saw men as basically divided into social classes based on their economic position. There was thus a landowning class and a class of landless peasants, a factory-owning class and a class of

A portrait of Karl Marx, who, with another German political thinker, Friedrich Engels, developed the philosophy of communism.

industrial workers — and, where it still existed, an aristocratic class and a class of serfs.

These classes had come into being naturally as a reflection of how men organized their means of livelihood over the centuries. History was, in fact, largely a record of the struggles between various of these classes for dominance in society. The Industrial Revolution had all but wiped out the aristocratic class and the serfs of feudal times, and the society of that time was composed, basically, of only two classes. These were the bourgeoisie, or middle-class owners of the means of production (factories, mines, transportation and communication systems, and so on), and the working classes, which owned only their own laboring power. These owners of the means of production, the bourgeoisie, exploited the workers for their own profit. Furthermore, political democracy, as it existed in England, France, or the United States, was only another means whereby the bourgeoisie exercised control of society. This economic system, based on the private ownership of the means of production, was called capitalism — and as a system, it was doomed; it would go the way of feudalism before it.

The new society predicted and advocated by Marx and Engels would be one in which the means of production would be owned by everyone communally. This economic system of the public ownership of the means of production was called socialism. It would better the lot of mankind because in it there would be neither exploiters nor exploited. "From each according to his ability, to each according to his needs" was to be its motto. Furthermore, socialism would give rise to true democracy because government would no longer be the expression of a single class, but the expression of the will of all.

28

How was this Socialist society to be established? Well, first of all, capitalism would die of its own inner contradictions. The bourgeoisie would grow richer and, as owners competed ruthlessly with each other, it would grow smaller as a class. In an ever more feverish race for raw materials and markets, bourgeois nations would fall into wars against each other. And all the while the working classes would grow ever larger and their lives ever more miserable until finally they would rise to take over society. But while this process was historically inevitable, it could be hastened and guided by the formation of strong working-class movements, which would struggle for power in their societies and prepare their members for eventual triumph. "Workers of the world, unite! You have nothing to lose but your chains," declared *The Communist Manifesto* issued by Marx and Engels in 1848.

But the last place in the world that the founders of communism would have expected a Socialist revolution was in the Russian Empire. This was because Russia was still, basically, a semifeudal society. No middle class worthy of the name existed; very little progress had been made toward industrialization, and hence there existed no large and politically educated working class. Russia would first have to pass through the stage of capitalism before there could be any question of Socialist revolution.

But Plekhanov insisted that special conditions in Russian history gave ground for hope. His Social Democratic party gained followers and, in 1903, held a conference in Brussels, Belgium (the party was, of course, illegal and officially banned in Russia). At this conference, leadership of the Social Democratic party passed into the hands of younger men, chief of whom was one Vladimir Ulyanov, known to history by his "underground" name of Lenin.

Lenin was born on April 22, 1870, into an upper-middle-class family in the provinces far from Moscow. He was a brilliant and determined student as a youth, overcoming many obstacles to win a law degree from St. Petersburg University in 1892. His student days were shadowed, however, by a tragedy that was to determine the course of his life. In 1887 Lenin's brother, Alexander Ulyanov, was arrested and hanged by the tsarist police for taking part in a student conspiracy to assassinate Tsar Alexander III (father of Nicholas II). It was this event that turned Lenin into an implacable foe of the tsarist autocracy and that led him to the study of Marxism as a possible means of bringing about its downfall.

In 1895 Lenin traveled to Switzerland, where he met Plekhanov and became a member of the Social Democratic party. Returning to Russia in that same year, he was imprisoned by the tsarist police for spreading Social Democratic propaganda and then sentenced to three years' exile in Siberia. During his exile he married a young fellow revolutionist, Nadezhda Krupskaya. When their term of exile ended in 1899, Lenin and Krupskaya returned to Switzerland, where they helped to edit the party newspaper, *Iskra* ("The Spark"), and spent the next few years in poverty-stricken wandering. By 1903, already acknowledged as the leader of the "young guard" among the Social Democrats, Lenin was ready to dispute party leadership with Plekhanov.

The issue that vexed the party conference in Brussels was whether the Social Democratic party should organize itself democratically, along traditional political party lines, or become a dictatorial, centralized party subject entirely to the direction of

30

its leaders. Lenin urged that only a small, secret, dictatorial, and utterly dedicated party could cope with the tsarist repression. He was against a democratic organization. By a very slim majority, Lenin's views prevailed at the conference. Therefore he and his followers claimed to be members of the *Bolshevik* ("majority") faction within the party, while their opponents were known as *Mensheviks* ("minority"). But despite this temporary victory in Brussels, it was actually the Mensheviks who had a large majority within the Social Democratic party — and the Mensheviks who largely controlled party affairs thereafter.

Taking little part in the party quarrel of 1903 was a young Russian intellectual named Lev Bronstein, who called himself Trotsky. He had gone through the same harsh school of police brutality, imprisonment, and exile as Lenin. But while he was a confirmed Marxist and Social Democrat, Trotsky refused to take sides at Brussels.

These interparty squabbles among the Social Democrats were interrupted in 1905 by the dramatic news that revolution

Lev Bronstein, who called himself Trotsky, as he appeared in later years.

had broken out in Russia. The party leaders in western European exile hurried home to help shape events. First to arrive was Trotsky, who immediately set about organizing the Petrograd workers into a Soviet that quickly won control of most of the city. Lenin placed himself at the head of the Moscow Soviet — but too late to prevent catastrophe. As we have seen, Tsar Nicholas II responded to the uprisings of 1905 by issuing a flood of promises. These promises seemed to satisfy many among the Russian middle classes and were even believed by many of the workers and peasants. As support for the uprisings waned, the tsar regained control of his mutinous army, and he used his elite guards regiments to savagely smash the Petrograd and Moscow Soviets. Thousands of workers were killed by the troops. Once again, Lenin and Krupskaya were forced to flee into exile in Switzerland, while Trotsky was arrested and deported again to Siberia.

After the disasters of 1905, the Social Democrats slowly rebuilt their organization. Trotsky escaped from Siberia by hiding under a wagonload of hay and made his way to Switzerland. There he found Lenin carrying on his endless theoretical feud with the Mensheviks. Over the coming years, the rift between Bolsheviks and Mensheviks in the Social Democratic party was to widen irreparably. The argument between them was basically whether or not Russia was ripe for a Socialist revolution. The Mensheviks, following a strict interpretation of Marxism, believed that a middle-class revolution followed by a development of capitalism would have to come before any Socialist revolution could succeed. Therefore, they held, the duty of the Social Democrats was to cooperate with liberal groups in hastening a democratic rather than a Socialist revolution.

As for Lenin and his Bolsheviks, they held that, first of all,

Two views of Lenin, whose real name was Vladimir Ulyanov. At left, Lenin is shown at the age of forty-seven, on the eve of the revolution. At right, he is shown in a typical pose while making a speech.

industrialization in Russia, while behind the West, was yet sufficiently advanced to provide a strong and self-aware working class. Secondly, the Russian middle classes were so weak and demoralized by the tsarist autocracy that it was hopeless to wait for them to make a revolution. When the people finally rose, they must be led straight into communism. Therefore, to cooperate with the liberal groups and parties in Russia was to betray the revolution. At committee meetings, party congresses, through underground party newspapers such as *Pravda* ("Truth"), and in countless pamphlets and books, Lenin hammered away at his thesis. While the Mensheviks continued to maintain a large majority within the Social Democratic party, by 1914 there were no less than thirty thousand Bolsheviks both in Russia and in exile committed to Lenin's ideas and leadership.

When world war broke out in 1914, a further split occurred among European Socialists. Marx had preached the international solidarity of all working classes. The Marxist view of the war was that it represented a fight for markets and raw materials among the capitalist nations — a fight from which only the bourgeoisie could gain while the workers were to be slaughtered. But European Socialists found reasons to betray this particular Marxist view and fight one another as supporters of their nations' war efforts. Lenin and a small group of followers would have none of this. They called upon the workers of all nations to turn the world war into civil war and revolution at home. But as the years of slaughter and destruction dragged by, it seemed to the Russian Socialist exiles in Switzerland that the revolution to which they had dedicated their lives was as far away as ever.

The First Revolution

What happened next came as a complete surprise — to the tsar and his ministers, to the revolutionary parties, even to the people themselves. The only group in all of Russia who expected something like the events of March, 1917, was the police — which was only natural, since they stood directly in the line of fire.

It started on March 8, International Women's Day. The women of Petrograd, however, did not feel much like celebrating. They toiled their usual twelve-hour day in the factories or waited in endless lines outside food stores hoping for the meager ration of bread with which to feed their families. Sometime during the day the women's patience became exhausted. The women workers at the textile mills spontaneously went out on strike. They were joined by the men of the giant Putilov metal factory. They formed a procession carrying hastily scrawled signs reading, "Down with the autocracy!" As they marched, they were joined by citizens of all kinds. And despite police cordons, more than ninety thousand marchers managed to reach the Nevsky Prospect, Petrograd's most fashionable street. They massed outside the building that housed the Duma and shouted for bread — a hopeless request.

The following day, the number of demonstrators doubled. And to the surprise of both the crowds and city officials, when squadrons of mounted cossacks were ordered to disperse the mobs, they refused. Not only that, but once when a policeman

35

The cossacks who joined forces with the Reds in Petrograd, March, 1917.

struck a woman with his club, a nearby cossack cut the police-man down with his saber! When twenty-five hundred strikers from the Erikson plants ran into a cossack squadron, the cossacks let them through. Kayurov, a Bolshevik worker, said, "Some of them [the cossacks] smiled and one of them gave the workers a good wink!" Evidently the cossacks, those ancient subduers of the people, the tsardom's most trusted defenders, were as sick of war, famine, and oppression as everyone else.

On March 10, no less than a quarter of a million people

thronged the streets of Petrograd. Police opened fire on them and were shot down by volleys from cossack rifles. When a group of workers to which Kayurov was attached was attacked by the police, he ran to a nearby cossack squadron. "Brothers — Cossacks, help the workers in a struggle for their peaceable demands; you see how the Pharaohs [a popular name for the police] treat us hungry workers. Help us!" The cossacks exchanged glances and then charged down upon the police. By the end of the day, the Petrograd police had gone into hiding.

On the same day, General Khabalov, military governor of Petrograd, called out the elite guards regiments stationed in the city. But these were no longer the professional soldiers of peacetime. These were draftee regiments, many of which had already been badly mauled at the front and were resting in Petrograd. Moreover, these regiments were composed of the sons, fathers, husbands, and brothers of the people demonstrating in the streets. They were peasants and workers themselves, and only fear of the punishment they could expect if the revolution failed held them to their duty.

By the morning of March 11, the crowds had armed themselves from the wreckage of police stations throughout the city. A three-day general strike had been proclaimed by a hastily organized meeting of Bolshevik, Menshevik, and other radical leaders, to whom the whole uprising had come as a stunning surprise. And, on March 11, the troops were ordered to open fire on the crowds. Some of the soldiers obeyed. Sixty workers were shot down by men of the Pavlovsky Regiment. But this incident only gave rise to angry arguments and fistfights among the troops themselves. That night, in the barracks that housed the Petrograd regiments, the talk grew hot. It was clear to the soldiers that

March 10, 1917. Tsarist troops open fire on workers in Petrograd.

the people were attempting to make a revolution. To shoot down the people meant shooting their own brothers, wives, sisters. By the dawn of March 12, the regiments had made their decision. Troops of the Moscow, the Volynsk, the Litovski, and the Pre-obrazhensky Regiments shot or imprisoned their officers and came out in favor of the revolution. With bands playing *La Marseillaise*, the soldiers marched out into the streets of Petrograd, led by armored cars carrying giant red banners — and with

38

their appearance all Petrograd fell into the hands of the revolutionary mobs.

Despite casualties of more than one thousand (mostly suffered early in the uprising at the hands of the police), the revolution had been so successful that many could not believe it. Certainly Tsar Nicholas II, at his headquarters at the front, did not believe it. When Khabalov telegraphed him for reinforcements on March 10, the tsar had replied, "I order that the disorders in the capital be stopped tomorrow!" ("I wish it; therefore it must be. . . .") But by March 12, General Khabalov was dolefully reporting that out of all the regiments and police forces in Petrograd, "I have at my disposal . . . four companies of the guard, five squadrons of cossack cavalry, and two batteries. . . . The rest of the troops have gone over to the revolutionists." Later, puzzling over the rapid evaporation of tsarist power, Khabalov mused about how he had sent troops out to crush the revolution. "The regiment starts . . . under a brave officer, but . . . there are no results." Yet how could there be results when the regiments were composed of the very peasants and workers who were supposed to be crushed?

On March 13, Tsar Nicholas, alarmed at last, set out on his private train to rejoin his family in Tsarskoe Selo, his summer palace outside Petrograd. But the railway workers were on the side of the revolution. They kept stopping and rerouting the tsar's train until they had forced it into a long and aimless journey all over the Russian countryside. As Trotsky later observed, "With its simple railroad pawns, the revolution had cried 'check' to the king!"

Meanwhile, in Petrograd, all eyes and hopes were focused on the Tauride Palace. In that venerable pile of masonry and stone sat the old Duma (shaking in their boots), and in another

39

Members of the tsar's secret police arrested by the revolutionaries in Petrograd.

wing of the same building, the new Petrograd Soviet met. This organization was hastily formed by leaders of all the revolutionary parties, including both Mensheviks and Bolsheviks, for the purpose of establishing a new government in Russia. N. N. Sukhanov, a Menshevik, described an early meeting of the Soviet: "Standing on stools, their rifles in their hands, agitated and stuttering, straining all their powers to give a concentrated account of the messages that had been given them . . . one after another the soldiers' deputies told of what was happening in their companies. . . . The audience listened as children listen to a wonderful, enthralling fairy tale they know by heart. . . . 'We had a meeting . . . we refuse to serve against the people anymore, we're going to join with our brother workers. . . . We would lay down our lives for that!' . . . Storms of applause. . . ."

The Soviet sent delegates to the city of Pskov, where the tsar's train had finally come to rest, to demand his abdication. Desperately trying to save his power, the tsar turned to his generals. But when one of them took a telephone poll of commanders at the German front, he found that all but one of the tsar's generals were mortally afraid of their own troops. The news of the revolution had reached the front — and the soldiers supported it to a man. The military leaders could offer no protection to the autocracy.

On the night of March 15, Nicholas II signed the document of abdication: "We have thought it good to abdicate from the throne of the Russian State, and to lay down the supreme power. . . . May the Lord God help Russia!" Later, after rejoining his family at Tsarskoe Selo, where they were all held under arrest by the revolutionary authorities, Nicholas complained, "There is no justice among men." But generations of untold millions of Russian peasants and workers would not have agreed with him. For the first time since Ivan the Terrible assumed the crown in 1547, there was no tsar in Russia.

Much later, when there was time for such things, historians would ask: "Who led the first revolution? Who organized it? How did it win apparently so easily and quickly?" Much would be made of its "spontaneous" nature — of the people themselves, fed up with war, famine, and oppression, rushing out into the streets to take matters into their own hands, and of the regiments joining them because they were, essentially, part of the people. Yet most of the factors present in 1917 had also been

41

Russian soldiers cheering the news of the overthrow of the tsar.

present in 1905, and at that time the revolution had failed abysmally. However, certain key things had changed since 1905.

First of all, the working class had been much enlarged. Russian industrialization had taken giant steps forward in the decade between the two revolutions. New factories had been opened and thousands of new workers had been recruited from the peasantry. These new factories had naturally been concentrated near and in the big cities, where there were prime sources of transportation, power, labor, and communications. So such centers as Petrograd, Moscow, and Kiev had a very much larger

42

working-class population in 1917 than they had had in 1905. Furthermore, the workers had had ten additional years of revolutionary propaganda drummed into their heads by secret "organizers" and agents of all the revolutionary parties.

Secondly, the tsarist autocracy had continued to decay from within. Nicholas, under the influence of his wife and Rasputin, had dismissed any ministers who displayed too much intelligence or determination. As the rumblings of discontent grew ever louder and nearer, the tsar and his government had come to rely more and more on naked police power to enforce their will. Perhaps subconsciously aware of their impending doom, the aristocrats gave themselves over increasingly to a life of aimless pleasure that would drown their fears.

And finally, the world war, by immeasurably increasing the strains on the tsarist government, exposed that regime's inefficiency and cruelty ever more clearly. The people were well aware that the millions of soldiers at the front had little equipment, that they were led by hopelessly incompetent generals, that they were simply being fed into the war as cannon fodder. And the soldiers themselves, having nothing but a reactionary tyranny to fight for, had grown heartily sick of the whole thing. One of the main reasons the Petrograd regiments joined the revolution was that they knew that, if the government was not changed, they would eventually be sent back to the front lines and to the slaughter. Likewise, the cossacks had been expended wastefully on the front lines — all the pressures felt by the average Russian soldier were felt equally by them. And, just as there were radical agents and organizers among the city workers, so among all the regiments and cossack squadrons there were men who had been politically "educated" by one or another of the revolutionary parties, who were eager to explain matters to their comrades, who would show them how to act effectively.

It may also be said that, despite the fact that almost all of the Menshevik, Bolshevik, and other radical leaders were either in exile or prison, their underground organizations and propaganda, given the massive discontent of the people, brought about the uprising that was only momentarily and superficially "spontaneous." And once it was under way, trained radicals of every revolutionary persuasion guided it. It was these men, surprised perhaps by their own success, who were now faced with the task of creating a new government upon the ruins of the tsardom.

The Struggle for Power

The basic paradox of Russian government in the months following the revolution was that political power was split between groups that did not really want it. Theoretically, the old Duma, dominated by liberal and conservative "bourgeois" parties, ruled the state. Its leaders formed the Provisional Government, and were to rule until a nationwide assembly of people's representatives could draft a constitution and decide on the final form of a new Russian government. But the Duma, and the so-called Provisional Government were, in actuality, all but powerless. Real political power rested with the Petrograd Soviet and its ruling executive committee. In other words, the vast masses of the people would only follow orders from or give their support to the Soviet. Only when the wishes of the Provisional Government and the Soviet coincided could the government be sure of popular support.

But the Petrograd Soviet was itself unwilling to take on the burdens of government. This was largely because the men who composed it were Mensheviks, Social Revolutionaries, and other (by Bolshevik standards) relatively conservative radicals. Faithful to their doctrine that Russia would have to go through a democratic-capitalist phase before any Socialist revolution, the majority of the members of the Soviet supported the Provisional Government and tried to encourage its middle-class parties to rule the state decisively.

After the revolution, all imperial eagles and other heraldic pomp reminiscent of tsarist rule were removed from public buildings.

Several difficult problems arose immediately, the most important of which was the question of war or peace. The government and the Soviet felt the need of continued Allied (British, French and, soon, American) support and recognition of the "legitimacy" of their rule. But the Allies were locked in a desperate life-and-death struggle with Germany. Only a Russian government that would continue to prosecute the war vigorously could hope for Allied support. Yet it was this very question of ending a disastrous war that had been central to the revolution. The people might continue to support the war effort for a while, to give their new government a chance to find an honorable way out — but not for long.

There were also the questions of land reform for the peasants and the reform of working conditions for the city laborers. There were signs that the peasants would wait no longer; if the new government did not immediately begin to parcel out the land to them, they would simply seize it on their own. The patience of the city workers was, likewise, not limitless. But the government was composed of the representatives of those classes such as middle-class factory owners and landowners, which would resist radical change. And the Soviet, in attempting to support these conservative classes, could only postpone and evade decisive action to meet the people's demands. It soon became apparent that the masses of the Russian people were far more radical than their radical leaders in the Soviet.

In the confusion and turmoil of the months following the revolution, the Bolshevik leaders in exile found their way back to Russia. Trotsky returned from the United States (he had been living in New York City) by way of a British prison, and Lenin from Switzerland in a sealed train supplied by the German government. (The Germans hoped Lenin's presence in Russia would help undermine the Russian war effort against them.)

When Lenin arrived in Petrograd, on April 16, 1917, he was met by an immense throng of soldiers, sailors, and workers. Speaking to them, he declared, "Dear comrades, soldiers, sailors, and workers. I am happy to greet in you the victorious Russian revolution, to greet you as the advance guard of the international proletarian [working-class] army. . . . The war of imperialist brigandage is the beginning of civil war in Europe. . . . The hour is not far when . . . the people will turn their arms against their capitalist exploiters. . . . Long live the International Social Revolution!"

"Suddenly," related N. N. Sukhanov, an observer of the

scene, "before the eyes of all of us, completely swallowed up by the routine drudgery of the revolution, there was presented a bright, blinding, exotic light." The light became even brighter when Lenin, speaking to his party comrades later, said, "We don't need any parliamentary republic. We don't need any bourgeois democracy. We don't need any government except the Soviet of Workers', Soldiers', and Peasants' Deputies!"

From that time forward, the Bolshevik party would pursue two aims: to force the Soviet to assume all the functions of government, and to win control of the Soviet itself.

The leading figure in the Provisional Government was Alexander Kerensky, a brilliant but wordy and weak-willed lawyer who was the only avowed Socialist in the government. When the government publicly promised the Allied powers that Russia would faithfully carry on the war and abide by all the old tsarist treaties, masses of people demonstrated in the streets of Petrograd. A witness of this event wrote, "Their faces amazed me. All those thousands had but one face, the stunned ecstatic face of the early Christian monks. Implacable, pitiless. . . ." These April demonstrations forced the Soviet to take more power in the Provisional Government and to disavow certain tsarist war aims.

In June, the Socialist parties held rival demonstrations in Petrograd. To the horror of the Mensheviks and conservative Socialists, Bolshevik masses, carrying Bolshevik banners and signs, completely dominated the gatherings. It was in June also that Kerensky and the Provisional Government, faithful to their obligations to the Allies, whipped the exhausted Russian armies into a new offensive against the Germans. But by July 16 this Russian offensive, predictably, had completely broken down and the Russian armies were once more reeling back in defeat.

Troops taking the oath of allegiance to the Provisional Government.

The disasters of the July offensive, combined with continued delay in reforms on the home front, provoked a spontaneous attempt on the part of the Petrograd workers to overthrow the Provisional Government in July. The Bolsheviks, fearing that this attempt was premature, tried to restrain the masses. Failing in this, they assumed leadership of the insurrection. But the Bolshevik leadership was right — the uprising was premature. It was put down bloodily by regiments loyal to the Provisional Government. For their unwilling part in it, the Bolsheviks were declared an outlaw party. Lenin, Trotsky, and other leaders were accused of being secret German agents who were trying to bring about Russian defeat. While Lenin escaped to Finland, Trotsky and others were imprisoned in the Fortress of Saints Peter and Paul.

Workers and soldiers invade the Duma, July, 1917.

Furthermore, it appeared that the masses of the people believed the charges against the Bolsheviks, so that by the end of July, 1917, the political power of Lenin's party seemed to have vanished.

But threats to the stability of the Provisional Government came not only from radicals; they came also from reactionaries — from those who hoped to restore the tsarist autocracy. The most dangerous of these threats was posed by ex-tsarist General Lavr Kornilov, commander in chief of the Russian armies. Kerensky hoped to use Kornilov's forces to destroy the power of the Petrograd Soviet, thereby leaving the Provisional Government supreme in Russia. But Kornilov, while pretending to agree with Kerensky, actually planned to destroy both the Soviet and the Provisional Government and effect a tsarist restoration.

50

While Kerensky and Kornilov plotted with and against each other, all the Socialist parties grew alarmed. The Petrograd Soviet secretly organized a military committee to defend the revolution. In doing so, they found that if they wanted the support of vital unions and key workers' groups, they would have to include many of the "outlawed" Bolsheviks. Having recovered their prestige among the people, after the disasters of July, by the end of August the Bolsheviks were once again a force to be reckoned with.

Early in September, 1917, Kornilov made his move. Divisions were sent from the front to "restore order" in Petrograd. The workers prepared to defend themselves. But as Kornilov's divisions advanced they were met by agitators sent out by the Soviet. "Almost everywhere," reported one of Kornilov's generals sadly, "we saw one and the same picture. On the tracks or in the [railway] cars, or in the saddles of their black or bay horses . . . dragoons would be sitting or standing, and in the midst of them, some lively personality in a soldier's long coat." That "lively personality" was the revolution's secret weapon — a man able to explain to the troops, in ways they could understand, just what it would mean to them to destroy the revolution. Like magic, Kornilov's forces seemed to melt away. His generals were arrested by their own men; some were hanged, some were shot, and some, like Kornilov himself, were made prisoner.

The Kornilov revolt mightily helped the cause of bolshevism throughout Russia. It was well known that Kerensky had first plotted with the general. It now appeared that all the Bolshevik accusations of corruption against the Provisional Government were true. Trotsky and other Bolshevik leaders were released from prison, and by the end of September, the Bolsheviks had won majorities in elections to the executive committees of the Petrograd, Moscow, and Kiev Soviets. The Bolshevik slogan during the summer had been "All Power to the Soviets!" Now they themselves had become the Soviets. Only Kerensky and his ghostly Duma-supported Provisional Government stood between the Bolsheviks and absolute power in Russia.

It was Lenin, analyzing events from his hideout in Finland, who pointed out to his followers in Petrograd that the time was ripe for a seizure of power. It was, he insisted, now or never. He pointed out that peasants throughout Russia under Social Revolutionary leadership were burning manor houses, taking over the land, and killing landlords. The Bolsheviks were, it was true, definitely in a minority in the countryside and out in the provinces. But the peasants and their Social Revolutionary leaders would, at this precise moment, support *any* national party which would sanction their land seizures. Social Revolutionaries would be invited to share power with the Bolsheviks, and after the revolution had triumphed, there would be time and means to deal with the rival peasant-based party. But if action were to be delayed, like the peasantry in other lands and other revolutions, once they had won the land, Russia's peasant millions would become conservative, attempting to hold onto their gains. In the same way, under the impact of the Kornilov rebellion, the city workers had flocked to the Bolshevik banners. Finally, because of the continuing horror of the war and the apparent refusal or inability of the Provisional Government to end it, the all-important armies were prepared to back the Bolsheviks.

Leon Trotsky, the energetic man-on-the-spot, was placed in tactical command of the coming insurrection. He worked with demonic energy to arm Red Guards detachments, and he laid

52

Red Guards patrolling the streets of Petrograd in November, 1917.

precise and careful plans. On October 23, Lenin returned secretly from Finland, disguised in a wig. On November 4, the Petrograd Soviet held large meetings of workers throughout the city at which they were addressed by Bolshevik orators. On November 5, Kerensky, now thoroughly alarmed, declared that an emergency existed and placed Petrograd under martial law. But most of the people of Petrograd simply paid no attention to Kerensky or his Provisional Government. Instead they flocked to the Bolshevik party headquarters at Smolny Institute (a former girls' school).

An American journalist, John Reed, was there to see. He wrote: "The long, vaulted corridors, lit by rare electric bulbs, were thronged with hurrying shapes of soldiers and workmen. . . . The sound of their heavy boots made a deep and incessant thunder on the wooden floor." Beneath that thunder the old

Russia was disappearing forever. When, months before, he had arrived in Petrograd, Lenin had told his party comrades, "We are not charlatans. We must base ourselves only upon the consciousness of the masses. . . . Our line will prove right. All the oppressed will come to us. . . . They have no other way out."

How and why had the Bolsheviks been able to win the masses to their cause? Because they were able to completely support the people's demands. Since they basically and theoretically felt no need for any stage of democratic-capitalist development in Russia, they had no need to support or compromise themselves with the Provisional Government. Since they were a party devoted exclusively to the interests of the workers, a party composed of professional revolutionaries with no stake whatsoever (in the form of wealth, ownership, or land) in the old social and economic order, they were free to advocate its complete destruction, to back the most extreme dreams and demands of the vast masses of the poor. And, because they believed in a worldwide, international revolution against all capitalist governments, they felt free to make peace at any price with the Germans — confident that no matter how harsh the terms might be for Russia, they would soon be swept away by a Socialist revolution in Germany itself. Thus they were able to promise the armies an end to the horror of war. The Bolshevik revolution in Russia, like all revolutions, took place in the consciousness of the people before it ever took place in the streets of the cities.

Nevertheless, also like other revolutions, the Bolshevik uprising in Russia would either succeed in the streets or it would be crushed in them. And as midnight neared on November 7, 1917, all streets in Petrograd seemed to lead to the great square before the Winter Palace. . . .

Epilogue:
Red Dawn—and Aftermath

As the heavy artillery of Saints Peter and Paul Fortress and the guns of the cruiser *Aurora* boomed out against the Winter Palace, both besiegers and besieged instinctively took cover. But out of thirty-five rounds fired at the huge structure at almost point-blank range, only two hit the building — and they only damaged some plaster. Was the aim of experienced naval gunners so bad? Or, even now, were the Bolshevik sailors and artillerymen reluctant to shed blood?

Effective or not, the bombardment convinced the volunteer Women's Battalion and most of the officer cadets to lay down their rifles in the great square before the palace and surrender. Emboldened now (and under imperative orders from Bolshevik headquarters at Smolny Institute), the Red Guards, armed workers, and sailors before the palace began to rush the entrances in larger and larger groups. Some officers inside the palace still stood guard. As small batches of workers and guards rushed in, they were arrested and disarmed. But nobody actually opened fire.

Now everything in the vast Winter Palace was confusion. Groups of Bolsheviks racing down dim corridors ran into groups of officers. Finally, the officers realized that they could no longer guard the large numbers of prisoners. Suddenly it was not even certain who was prisoner and who was captor. Both defenders and attackers became hopelessly mixed up. Huge throngs of

Above, Russian revolutionary soldiers attacking the Winter Palace on November 8, 1917. Right, the red flag has just been hoisted atop this portion of the Winter Palace on November 8.

workers and sailors then poured into the palace, flowing up grand staircases, down dusty corridors, into ornate rooms of state. At last the crowd reached the door of an inner chamber. Within sat the Provisional Government. The crowd burst in.

"In front of the crowd," one minister later recalled, "and trying to hold back the onpressing ranks, strode a rather small, unimpressive man. His clothes were all in disorder, a wide-brimmed hat askew on his head, eyeglasses balanced uncertainly on his nose, but his little eyes gleamed with the joy of victory. . . ." This individual was Antonov, a naval ensign from the *Aurora*. He announced to the assembled ministers of the Provisional Government that they were under arrest. The gilded clock in the Malachite Chamber pointed to 2:10 A.M., the morning of November 8, 1917.

A few hours after the fall of the Winter Palace, Lenin appeared in public for the first time since his escape to Finland the previous August. He was to address a meeting of the All-Russian Congress of Soviets, which was in session even as the Bolsheviks seized power. John Reed reported: "Now Lenin, gripping the edge of the reading stand, let little winking eyes travel over the crowd as he stood there waiting, apparently oblivious to the long-rolling ovation. . . . When it had finished he said simply, 'We shall now proceed to construct the socialist order.' Again that overwhelming human roar."

And so it was to be — although it was not perhaps as simple and immediately decisive as Lenin had assumed. While there was almost no bloodshed in Petrograd, Bolshevik forces had to fight hard battles in Moscow and Kiev to win control. And ahead lay long months and years of a terrible, bloody civil war between Bolshevik forces and armies commanded by various tsarist generals (sometimes with the support and aid of the Allies, who were soon to intervene in Russian affairs). Nevertheless, from all these trials, the Bolsheviks (now calling themselves the Communist party of the Soviet Union) were to emerge triumphant. Would they keep the promises that had won them victory?

Certainly they succeeded in putting an immediate end to the war. Within six months of the Bolshevik uprising, Russia had signed a separate peace treaty with Germany. Its terms were very harsh; yet, in a sense, Lenin proved correct. The terms of the Brest-Litovsk Treaty were swept away and obliterated both by the Allied victory over Germany and by the chaotic confusion that gripped postwar Europe.

And, at first, the peasants were encouraged in their seizure of the land. It was, of course, only a matter of years before their newly won land would be taken away from them, to be turned into gigantic state farms and collectives by the government, upon which they would be forced to work as farm laborers.

As for the working classes, they certainly won immediate power with the Bolshevik victory — factories, mines, transportation and communications systems, all the "means of production" were taken over and their former private owners kicked out. But it seemed that it was still the government, not the workers directly, who would henceforth manage Russian industry. Thus, in a sense, the workers simply exchanged one set of masters for another.

What of political democracy? This did not exist even temporarily. Not only was it always the Bolshevik intention to establish a "dictatorship of the proletariat [working classes]," but also it is hard to see how any other form of government could have emerged from Lenin's dictatorially organized, conspiratorial party. Political democracy was not part of the Bolshevik tradition — and, perhaps more importantly, it had never been part of the Russian experience. Despite the eventual establishment of a constitution (theoretically, one of the world's "freest"), the new Union of Soviet Socialist Republics would remain a dictatorship of the Communist party over the people — and of the leaders of the party machine over the government itself. All too soon, the entire apparatus of tsarist repression, including the dreaded secret police, Siberian labor camps, and so forth, was to be resurrected in an even more frighteningly efficient form.

Yet, through unbelievable sacrifice, terrible tyranny, and an all but religious fanaticism, within a quarter of a century Communist rule in Russia was to accomplish the transformation of that backward land into a modern industrial state. It was to produce the armies that defeated a later and far more dangerous German war machine; to make Russia the second most industrialized nation on earth; to develop the education and science that would one day lead mankind into outer space; to make the USSR, with the United States, one of the two sole world superpowers.

In addition, the success of the Bolshevik undertaking in Russia was to inspire later Communist revolutions all over the world. Sometimes "spontaneously" (as in the case of China, Yugoslavia, and Cuba), sometimes under the guns of the Red Army (as in much of Eastern Europe), Communist parties would arise and seize power over the years ahead until nearly one-third of mankind lived under their rule.

And the principal actors in the drama of the November revolution? Most of the Provisional Government ministers were to end their lives in exile. Premier Alexander Kerensky would pass his days as a professor of Political Science at an American university. Nikolai Lenin, first premier of the new Soviet state, would die prematurely in 1924, with the mantle of his leadership passing to an obscure party functionary named Josef Djugashili who called himself Stalin ("man of steel"). Stalin would erect a tyranny in Russia the like of which had not been seen since the days of Ivan the Terrible. Leon Trotsky, tactician of the Bolshevik triumph, would eventually be exiled by Stalin and later murdered in Mexico by a Stalinist agent. The tsar and all his family would be executed by frightened Red Guards during the years of civil war that followed the fall of the Winter Palace.

All of these events, of course, lay hidden in the future on that cold November morning in 1917. In fact, most of Petrograd remained unaware that an event of earth-shaking consequences had taken place. Many did not know that the Bolsheviks had seized power; and among those who did, none could have foreseen all the historical ramifications. Reflecting on the events of November 7 and 8 many years later, Leon Trotsky was to write: "The bourgeois classes had expected barricades, flaming conflagrations, looting, rivers of blood. In reality a silence reigned more terrible than all the thunders of the world. The social ground shifted noiselessly like a revolving stage, bringing forward the popular masses, carrying away into limbo the rulers of yesterday."

Chronology

1237–1240 – Mongol hordes bloodily conquer European Russia.

1547 – Ivan IV ("the Terrible") proclaims himself first tsar of Russia.

1552 – Ivan IV conquers Mongol fortress of Kazan and breaks Mongol power.

1768 – Empress Catherine the Great begins First Turkish War.

1812 – Tsar Alexander I defeats Napoleon's invasion of Russia and later leads his conquering armies to Paris.

1825 – The "Decembrists'" attempt to overthrow the tsarist autocracy is crushed by Tsar Nicholas I.

1856 – Russia is humiliatingly defeated by England and France in the Crimean War.

1848–1890 – Marx and Engels publish their most important theoretical works defining the Communist political-economic philosophy.

1881 – Tsar Alexander II assassinated by revolutionaries.

1887 – Alexander Ulyanov, Lenin's brother, is hung by order of Tsar Alexander III for taking part in a revolutionary conspiracy.

1898 – The Russian Social Democratic (Marxist) party is secretly founded by Georgi Plekhanov.

1903 – Lenin establishes the Bolshevik wing of the Social Democratic party while young corevolutionary Trotsky stands aloof from party squabbles.

1905 – Russia is defeated in a war against Japan. Uprisings occur throughout Russia. Trotsky heads the revolutionary government of Petrograd while Lenin leads the workers of Moscow.

1906 – The revolution of 1905 is finally stamped out by Tsar Nicholas II; Lenin and Trotsky flee into exile.

1914 – Russia enters World War I as an ally of Britain and France against Imperial Germany and Austria-Hungary.

1914–1917 – Russian armies are catastrophically defeated by the Germans.

1916 – The evil monk Rasputin, adviser of the royal family, is murdered by frightened aristocrats.

March, 1917 – The people of Petrograd, joined by army regiments, topple the tsarist autocracy. Nicholas II abdicates. A new, democratic Provisional Government is established.

April, 1917 – Lenin returns from exile, calls for the abolition of the new Provisional Government and the establishment of a workers', peasants', and soldiers' "democratic dictatorship."

June, 1917 – Trotsky returns from exile. Rival mass demonstrations in Petrograd reveal surprising Bolshevik power among the workers.

July, 1917 – Premier Kerensky's ill-advised offensive against the Germans collapses in defeat. Petrograd workers attempt to topple the Provisional Government, but are defeated. The Bolshevik party is outlawed; Trotsky imprisoned, Lenin forced to flee to Finland.

September, 1917 – General Kornilov attempts a counterrevolution but is defeated. The Bolsheviks, resurgent, win control of many local Soviets (councils).

October, 1917 – The Bolsheviks, led by Trotsky and guided by
Lenin from exile, arm and plan to seize power.

November, 1917 – The Bolsheviks, led by Trotsky and Lenin,
seize control of Petrograd, overthrow the Provisional Government, and declare themselves the government of Russia.

Suggested Reading

Crossman, Richard (ed.) *The God That Failed*. New York: Harper, 1949.

Denikin, Anton I. *The White Army*. New York, 1930.

Fischer, Louis. *The Life of Lenin*. New York: Harper, 1964.

Kerensky, Alexander F. *The Kerensky Memoirs*. New York, 1965.

Koestler, Arthur. *Darkness at Noon*. New York, 1940.

Kropotkin, Peter A. *Memoirs of a Revolutionist*. Boston, 1899.

Lockhart, Robert H. B. *Memoirs of a British Agent*. New York: Putnam, 1933.

Mehring, Franz. *Karl Marx*. New York, 1953.

Moorehead, Alan. *The Russian Revolution*. New York: Harper, 1958.

Wilson, Edmund. *To the Finland Station*. New York: Doubleday, 1940.

Index